The Perfect Shot: Mini Edition for Africa

Kevin "Doctari" Robertson

Safari Press Inc.
P. O. Box 3095, Long Beach, CA 90803

To our daughters, Samantha, Natalie, and Purdey.
May the wild places of Africa and the game animals therein be enjoyed by your children's children.

Robertson, Kevin

Second edition

Safari Press Inc.

2003, Long Beach, California

ISBN 1-57157-319-4

Library of Congress Catalog Card Number: 99-71150

10 9 8 7 6 5 4 3 2

Readers wishing to receive the Safari Press catalog, featuring many fine books on big-game hunting, wingshooting, and sporting firearms, should write to Safari Press Inc., P.O. Box 3095, Long Beach, CA 90803, USA. Tel: (714) 894-9080 or visit our Web site at www.safaripress.com.

CONTENTS

ACKNOWLEDGMENTS

To my wife Catherine, for her wonderful photographs and ideas, as well as her continuous love, support, and encouragement, and to Cathy Nel, our friend and neighbour, for her artwork and infinitely patient desire to "get it all right."

ABBREVIATIONS AND REFERENCES

Throughout the text and appendices of this book, Safari Club International's *SCI Record Book of Trophy Animals* is abbreviated as *SCI* and *Rowland Ward's Records of Big Game* is abbreviated as *RW*. An explanation of SCI and RW measurement methods (referred to throughout text as numbers in parentheses) is given in Appendices II and III.

INTRODUCTION

"Within reason, where you hit a game animal is more important than what you hit it with" is an often-quoted and very true statement. And the reason for it is simple—correct first shot placement, with a suitably sized, adequately constructed bullet, is, without a doubt, the most important criterion for successful, and therefore enjoyable, sport hunting, regardless of the species concerned.

To accomplish this, a thorough knowledge of any game animal's sex, habits, and habitat is essential. Even more so is knowing the internal bodily positions of all the "vital for immediate life" organs—the heart, lungs, brain, and spinal column—from all angles.

It is, therefore, my hope that this booklet will serve to illustrate this to the sport hunter of African game animals and, in so doing, help him or her to do so well, enjoyably, and ethically.

Elephant

Fully broadside. The best position for both the high heart/lung and the brain shot.

THE AFRICAN ELEPHANT

Loxodonta africana

Natural History — Member of Big Five. World's largest land mammal. Weighs up to seven tons, stands eleven feet or more at the shoulder. Dark gray skin provides excellent camouflage. Extremely nimble and fast for its size. Eyesight relatively poor, sense of smell phenomenal, hearing also very good. Life expectancy 50 to 70 years. Voracious and destructive feeders. Preferred diet: grass. Daily food requirement: 500 pounds.

Sex Determination — Cows found in herds of varying size; smaller body size; thin, slender tusks; sharp, almost 90-degree angle to foreheads. Mature bulls have large heads in relation to body size, top of forehead rounded, not angled. Usually found on their own or in company of a few other bulls, only occasionally with a herd of cows. Tuskless cows and those with young calves at side can be extremely aggressive.

Trophy Assessment — The older the elephant, the better. Cracks on the soles of the feet widen and deepen with age, and heels (hind feet especially) wear smooth when old. Soles of front feet round, hind feet oval. Judging weight of ivory: Estimate diameter of tusk at lip in inches x 3 = circumference of tusk at lip. Multiply this by estimated length of tusk along outside of curve, from lip to tip, in feet. Subtract 5 and answer will be tusk's approximate weight in pounds. SCI method (14): sum of weight of both tusks. RW method (16) weight of heaviest tusk.

The Hunt — Involves finding the right spoor and then tracking. You hunt an elephant with your legs! Toenail scuffmarks point forward, indicating direction of travel. Spoor size indicates body size and also age. Droppings are used to determine how close you are getting. Fresh dung strong smelling, warm, wet, and yellowish green in color; changes to walnut brown as outer surface dries out. Wind direction very important. Move slowly and quietly. Get in close for the first shot. Fifty paces is considered a long shot; 20–30 about average.

Rifle, Calibre, and Bullet Selection — Legal minimum .375 H&H. Use only good-quality solids. No margin for shot placement error with .375. The various .40 calibres and 400-grain solids a better option; more knock-down effect. The .458s and 500-grain solids at a minimum of 2100 fps the best choice.

Shot Placement — Broadside high heart/lung shot safest and surest: Sight up back edge of front leg, then up armpit crease to where it stops; a hand's width above this point and a hand's width in front of it is top of heart. Full frontal heart/lung shot possible only if elephant has trunk out of the way and head up: Place shot squarely into centre of chest. Brain shot: Impressive but difficult for the inexperienced to get angles right. Side-on brain shot easier: Place in ear hole or up to a hand's width in front of it (remember to compensate for upward shooting angle if head held higher than shooter's eye level). Frontal brain shot difficult; depends entirely on angle of head: Imagine a broomstick through ear holes; shoot to cut broomstick in half. Backup shots: Spinal shot best option from rear, or try to break either of the hip joints. Raking body shot best when angled away. Get in as many backup shots as possible—just in case.

The Perfect Shot: Mini Edition for Africa

Anatomy diagram

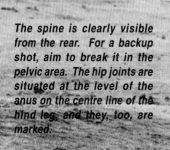

The spine is clearly visible from the rear. For a backup shot, aim to break it in the pelvic area. The hip joints are situated at the level of the anus on the centre line of the hind leg, and they, too, are marked.

The full frontal brain shot. From this angle, the zygomatic bulges are at eye level with the imaginary broomstick through the head and out the ear holes. From such a position, this elephant's brain would be above the hunter's eye level. A shot placed as indicated, level with the bottom of the eyes, would need to angle upward slightly to find the brain and cut the broomstick in half.

Elephant

The fully broadside shot. This bull was running when the photo was taken, so right front leg is positioned farther forward than it would be when standing. The aiming points for the high heart/lung, the high shoulder/spinal, and the neck/spinal shots are indicated.

BUFFALO
Syncerus caffer

Natural History — One of the Big Five. A dangerous game animal; aggressive, vindictive, cunning. Cape buffalo can weigh up to three-quarters of a ton; exceptional eyesight, hearing, and sense of smell. Gregarious herd animals. Water-dependent coarse grazers; occasional browsers. Favor thick bush during daylight. Ruminants. Five subspecies are recognized

Sex Determination — Can be difficult when visibility restricted. Both sexes carry horns, but cows do not have a boss. Mature bulls have thick, well-muscled necks, heavy, well-developed shoulders, blunt horn tips, a solid boss, and a distinctly visible penis sheath.

Trophy Assessment — Look for wide outside spread, deep curl, and a solid boss. SCI method (4): sum of length in inches of both horns around the outside of the curl, combined with straight-line width of both bosses; only bulls may be entered. RW method (12): width of outside spread. When a mature bull is looking at you, outside spread of ear tips = 30–32 inches. A hand's width (4 inches) of spread beyond the ear tips on both sides = +/- 40-inch bull, RW measurement. With a solid boss, this is a good trophy.

The Hunt — Track, walk, and stalk. Buffalo need to drink daily; makes finding spoor easier. Warmth and freshness of dung good indicator of how far ahead they are. Watch/listen for oxpeckers, the hunter's friend.

Rifle, Calibre, and Bullet Selection — Shooting distances are usually short (20–120 paces) with majority of shots taken at 30–80 paces. Legal minimum is 9.3x62mm, 9.3x74R, or .375 H&H, depending on country. Larger calibres, .40s and .458s, more effective. Premium-quality expanding bullets for initial, well-positioned shots; solids for all backing ones. Good-quality, low-power or 1–4X variable scope an advantage.

Shot Placement — Side-on high heart/lung shot the surest/most recommended: Place shot into centre of the "vital triangle." Side-on neck/spinal shot: Place shot just in front of and a hand's width (4 inches) above point of shoulder. Side-on shoulder/spinal shot: Place shot higher up on shoulder, through neck or shoulder blade. Full frontal chest shot: Place shot squarely into centre of chest at shoulder-joint level. Full frontal spinal shot: Place shot below the chin, into centre of neck. Full frontal brain shot: Take only if really close; just where depends on angle of head. (Nose up: Place shot on bridge of nose between top of nostrils and below eyes. Nose down: Place shot just below boss.) Full frontal neck shot (when buffalo is facing you with head down): Place shot into back of neck anywhere along the centre line. Quartering frontal shot: Depends on angle; place either on shoulder joint or just inside it. Quartering-away shots: Should be taken only as backup shots. Remember: Rumen situated on left-hand side. Rear end or "Texas heart shot": Most common backup shot; place fairly high up, just above the anus at the base of the tail.

Buffalo

Broadside anatomy diagram. Notice the broad, overlapping ribs, the top of the heart in the centre of the vital triangle, and the lungs not extending all that far rearward.

Buffalo

The frontal shot. This bull is quartering slightly. To compensate for the angle, both the top-of-the-heart/lung and the neck/spinal shots should be placed just off-centre. With the muzzle neither lifted nor "pointed," a shot just above eye level would find the brain.

Frontal anatomy diagram. Notice the centrally situated heart and how low the spinal column dips beneath the chin.

Fully broadside, the round shape and blubbery skin of a mature bull hippo conceal the shoulder and front leg bones, making the vital triangle difficult to distinguish. The high heart/lung, shoulder/spinal, and neck/spinal shots are marked.

Hippopotamus

HIPPOPOTAMUS

Hippopotamus amphibius

Natural History — *Hippopotamus* in Greek means "river or water horse." Four distinct toes on each foot. Herbivores. Live 30 to 40 years. Nocturnal grazing animals; leave the safety of water to graze at night. Front teeth are for threatening displays and fighting. Bristle-covered lips used for grazing. Can weigh up to three tons, consume in excess of one hundred pounds of herbage per night. Social animals; found in pods that average ten to fifteen members. Not good swimmers; run along bottom instead. Can run eighteen miles per hour on land. When surprised there, they head for safety of deep water by shortest possible route; dangerous when they do so. Kill more African natives than all other dangerous game animals put together. Cows with young calves especially dangerous; approach with extreme caution.

Sex Determination — Mature bulls have broader, longer, and generally bigger heads in relation to overall body size; necks also thicker and more muscular. When they are submerged, the only way to determine sex is to observe the pod carefully. Dominant bull will usually be on its fringes, performing threatening displays. Compare head sizes carefully.

Trophy Assessment — A hippo's tusks (two lower incisor teeth) are its most impressive and recordable trophies. Field judging of trophy quality difficult as half of tusk's length embedded in jawbone. SCI method (12): sum of length of both tusks + circumference of both tusks at largest place. RW method (5): length of longest tusk.

The Perfect Shot: Mini Edition for Africa

The Hunt — Usually illegal to hunt at night or with use of spotlight. Also considered unethical to shoot at or within a reasonable distance of any permanent water source or from a boat. Since hippo usually found in or next to water during legal shooting hours, hunter's own conscience is deciding factor. Not easy to approach on land; have good eyesight, keen sense of hearing, relatively good sense of smell. Ambushing basking bank or stalking an identified bull as it basks in the sun are the most ethical hunting methods. Many wounded hippo are lost if they get back to flowing water.

Rifle, Calibre, and Bullet Selection — Hippo are huge and thick skinned. Legal minimum is .375 H&H or the various 9.3mms, which also generate in the region of 4,000 ft-lb of muzzle energy. Larger calibres more effective for body shots, but not as accurate for brain ones. Good-quality solids for all body shots; premium-quality softs for brain shots. A suitable scope essential for precise shot placement required for brain shots.

Shot Placement — Side-on high heart/lung shot, most effective if far from running water: Come up back edge of front leg and place shot between one-third and halfway up the body on that line. Shoulder spinal shot: Place shot right on shoulder joint. Side-on brain shot best to "anchor" hippo: Place shot at base of ear or at that level but an inch or two in front of it. Frontal chest shot impossible when head is down; brain shot only option to stop a charge.

The Perfect Shot: Mini Edition for Africa

Hippopotamus

In the frontal head-down position, the inverted V formed by the hippo's bulging eye sockets is easy to see. The front edge of the brain reaches to the base of the V.

Hippopotamus

From the rear, the spine is still visible under the thick skin. Place a stopping shot as indicated. Notice the large fight wound on this bull's flank—probably the reason he is out of the water during the heat of the day.

Hippopotamus

A white rhino, fully broadside—the ideal position for a high heart/lung shot.

RHINOCEROS

Ceratotherium simum (White), *Diceros bicornis* (Black)

Natural History — One of the Big Five. *Ceratotherium simum*—white or square-lipped rhinoceros; *Diceros bicornis*—black or hooked-lip rhino. White considerably larger than black, longer, broader, more prehistoric-looking head with broad muzzle, prominent hump in the neck and shoulder region. Weigh as much as 2½ tons. Exclusively grazing animals, grass only diet; lifespan up to 40 years. Social and relatively docile; aggressive only when actively courting or protecting young. Black rhino smaller in overall body size (a mature bull will weigh about a ton) with smaller, shorter head, rounder ears, distinct prehensile or hooked upper lip. Almost exclusively woody browsers. More temperamental than the white, may charge without provocation. Both types of rhino carry two continuously growing "horns," dense, hairlike skin outgrowths.

Sex Determination — White rhino difficult, as some mature females attain the huge size of old males. Females' horns may be longer than males', but usually more slender, with smaller bases. Behaviour upon defecation and urination is also a key. Checking the area below the tail is the best way to be certain of a rhino's sex.

Trophy Assessment — SCI method (8): length of both horns + circumference of both horns at bases. RW method (15): length of longest horn. Horn length of 25 inches = good, 28 inches = excellent.

The Hunt — Trophy fee approximately U.S.$30,000; white rhino most expensive of Big Five. Classified as dangerous but relatively docile. Dominant breeding bulls are strongly territorial, walk the same well-worn paths. Spoor large and easy to find on well-worn game trails and dirt tracks. Grazing animals. Spend the first and last few hours of daylight feeding out in the open; easy to spot from a distance. Have phenomenal hearing, well-developed sense of smell, but poor eyesight. Relatively easy to approach to within fifty paces. Must be done quietly and slowly, from downwind.

Rifle, Calibre, and Bullet Selection — Rhino are considered pachyderms with good reason. Their skin is incredibly thick. Only the very best-quality solid bullets should be used, regardless of calibre. For quick and effective high heart/lung shots (the only shot recommended for a rhino), the .375 H&H and good 300-grain solids are as low as one can legally go. Larger calibres are more effective.

Shot Placement — High heart/lung shot from full broadside position is shot of choice: Come up centre of foreleg until you reach a point about ten inches above the prominent skin fold, then shift point of aim rearward about six inches. Quartering frontal shot: Place shot inside the point of the shoulder at that level. Brain shot only on charging rhino. Backup shots usually taken from the rear-end position: Place shot in centre above root of tail.

The Perfect Shot: Mini Edition for Africa

Anatomy diagram of a white rhino

The head of a black rhino is considerably shorter and smaller than that of a white rhino. Notice the prehensile or hooked upper lip.

Anatomy diagram of a black rhino. A limited number of black rhino may soon be made available to trophy hunters in South Africa.

Rhinoceros

From the side, the full mane of a trophy lion may cover the shoulder area, making the high shoulder/spinal shot difficult. From this position and angle, a high heart/lung shot is the obvious choice. The aiming points for the high heart/lung and the shoulder/spinal shots are indicated.

Lion

LION
Panthera leo

Natural History — One of the Big Five; Africa's most well-known, respected, and feared dangerous big-game animal; largest of Africa's felines. Weighs between 400 and 500 pounds, stands nearly four feet at shoulder, overall length up to ten feet. Lionesses are somewhat smaller, weighing 250 to 350 pounds. Generally more aggressive than males. Mature lion have little fear of man; especially bold during darkness. Superb night vision. Lionesses with cubs particularly aggressive. Lion prey on virtually all of the continent's animal species. Retractable, talon-like claws. Only members of cat family that live social lives.

Sex Determination — Only males have manes; mane starts to develop between 2½ and 3 years. Some males remain maneless but are generally larger than females with thicker, heavier-set necks and more heavily muscled shoulders.

Trophy Evaluation — Mane on exceptional lion will cover the shoulders and frontal chest area. May even extend down to the elbows and along belly line. Skull measured for record book; SCI method (15) and RW method (17): combined score in inches of greatest length and width of skull.

The Hunt — Baiting is most commonly practiced lion hunting method. Lion have huge appetites; can consume up to 25 percent of own body weight in single feeding. Need large quantities of meat for baiting purposes.

Zebra favorite bait, followed by buffalo and hippo, but will feed on virtually any kind of meat. Hang bait at least six feet above ground from a tree in the centre of an open area with good, all-round visibility. Lion will usually feed on bait during the hours of darkness. Catch them still on it at first light (half-hour before sunrise) or when they arrive at last light. Tracking lion not all that difficult—like to walk on roads and game trails. Tracking to daytime resting place also a good hunting method.

Rifle, Calibre, and Bullet Selection — A 7mm that produces 3,000 ft-lb of muzzle energy the legal minimum in some African countries. In others, .375 H&H. With smaller calibres, use heaviest softpoint bullet available. With larger calibres, softpoint bullets that will expand relatively quickly are the ones of choice. Good scope essential for all "bait"/low-light shots. Wounded lion follow-up entirely different situation. For this, bigger is definitely better: .40 or .458 calibres with heavy, expanding bullets. Open, express-sighted double the best rifle choice for a follow-up.

Shot Placement — Side-on high heart/lung shot surest and most recommended: Place shot well back behind shoulder, on or just below the body's horizontal midline. High shoulder/spinal shot will drop a lion; the spine lies directly beneath middle of shoulder blade. With trophy lion that are not heavily maned, sometimes possible to make out scapula beneath skin; however, when mane covers shoulders, this shot extremely difficult. Brain shot not recommended as skull measured for record books. Full frontal shot: Place shot squarely into centre of chest. Rear-end shot: Place at base of tail just above anus; never an initial shot, only as back up.

The Perfect Shot: Mini Edition for Africa

Broadside anatomy diagram. Notice how low and far to the rear the heart is situated.

Place a shot from the full frontal position squarely into the centre of the chest. The shock from the right calibre and bullet should crumple a lion.

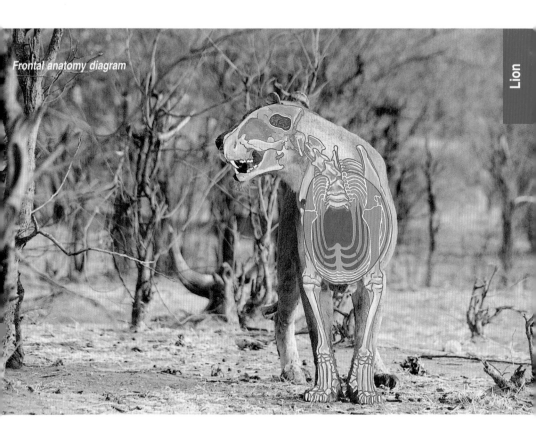

Frontal anatomy diagram

A good tom leopard. Notice his large overall size and well-muscled neck and shoulders. When the front leg is in its most rearward position while walking, the point of the elbow covers the bottom of the heart. The aiming points for the high heart/lung and the shoulder/spinal shots are indicated.

Leopard

LEOPARD
Panthera pardus

Natural History — Smallest in body size and most widely distributed of Africa's Big Five; most dangerous when wounded. Solitary animals, live in isolation. Shy and secretive, primarily nocturnal. Can live without water if necessary by getting their moisture requirements from prey but will drink regularly if water available. Mature tom weighs between 120 and 180 pounds, female 70 to 130 pounds. Can consume as much as 20 percent of body weight at a single sitting. Strongly territorial. Effective and ruthless killers. Prey on virtually any meat source; also scavenge; like rotten meat. Life expectancy 12 to 15 years.

Sex Determination — Difficult. Mature toms large, thickset, and well muscled. Heads larger in relation to overall size. Mature females slender, not as well muscled; heads smaller, thinner necks. Male and female rarely seen together, so difficult to compare.

Trophy Assessment — Body length (nose to tip of tail) used to determine size. Any tom >7 feet = good trophy; any tom >8 feet = huge. Size of spoor an aid to determining body size. Trophy leopard's spoor will be 3½ to 4 inches in length. Mature male nearly always has largest spoor; set up bait near its tracks. SCI method (15) and RW method (17): combined score in inches of skull's length and greatest width.

Leopard

The Hunt — Search for suitably sized spoor in areas where favored prey most abundant—near water holes, pans, river pools; select suitable blind site (be able to get in and out unseen), and hang bait. Bait tree not too exposed. Easy access to blind most important. Impala usually make best bait; also warthog, bushpig. Drag bait area well, but do not overdo "scent." Build blind 50–120 paces downwind of bait once it has been fed on. Stable shooting rest in blind most important. Sit still; leopard have phenomenal eyesight and hearing. Communicate only by gestures. In dry, sandy areas, tracking also used as a hunting method.

Rifle, Calibre, and Bullet Selection — A 7mm is as low as one should go. In some African countries various 9.3mms or .375 H&H are minimum legal calibres for all dangerous game, including leopard. Bullets suitable for leopard should be relatively light and fairly fragile so as to rapidly release kinetic energy (hydrostatic shock). A good-quality, light-gathering scope with bold, easily visible, or illuminated reticle essential.

Shot Placement — Leopard particularly susceptible to hydrostatic shock. Heart positioned well back in chest cavity. Side-on high heart/lung shot very effective: Place shot halfway up body, above where elbow reaches when front leg is at its most rearward position while walking. High shoulder/spinal shots, used to "drop" a leopard, good choice for "last light" situations. Standing side-on shoulder/spinal shot: Place shot through centre of shoulder blade. Also good option when leopard in "dog sitting" position. Quartering, frontal shot: Place right on shoulder joint. Full-frontal shot: Place squarely into centre of chest. Quartering-away shots: Aim to break opposite shoulder. Shots taken at leopard lying on a branch or on the ground are not recommended.

Leopard

Side-on "walking" anatomy diagram

Leopard

A good tom, perfectly broadside in the "dog sitting" position. The high shoulder/spinal shot is the best one to take, or place a high heart/lung shot in the centre of the body along the back edge of the front legs; either should drop the cat.

Leopard

"Dog sitting" anatomy diagram

Leopard

From the side, the corner of the croc's mouth forms an L-shaped "smile." The golf-ball-sized brain lies midway between the eye and the ear ridge, an inch or two above the bend in the L. A shot placed a couple of inches beyond the tip of the smile will break the neck and sever the spinal cord where the skull joins the neck.

Crocodile

NILE CROCODILE
Crocodylus niloticus

Natural History — One of Africa's most unusual trophies. Known locally as *ngwena,* "crocs," "flat dogs," or simply "flatties." Shy, wary, and cautious, egg-laying reptiles; cold-blooded. Nocturnal feeders; spend hours of darkness in water. Diet primarily fish. Bask in sun to "re-energize." Long-living, slow-growing creatures. Trophy-sized specimens will be 75 to 100 years old. Bull crocodiles are territorial. Patrol territories regularly. Extremely difficult to approach on foot to within a reasonable shooting distance.

Sex Determination — With young crocodiles, virtually impossible; easier with trophy-sized crocs. Big bull crocodile will have a large, noticeably broad head and wide, well-rounded, V-shaped muzzle. Entire head will have a knobby appearance, gums receded, teeth distinctly visible. Neck thick, broad, and muscular, with well-developed, fleshy jowls to the sides. Eyes relatively far apart. Female's head more slender, muzzle parallel sided. Females rarely longer than 12 feet.

Trophy Assessment — Difficult to estimate body length accurately. A really big croc will just look "big"; back and neck extremely wide; large and round belly; fleshy, well-developed jowls. Estimate straight-line length, in inches, from nostrils to eyes; this length in inches approximately equal to total body length in feet. Regardless of sex, 12 feet = good trophy, >13 feet = really good, >14 feet = exceptional, >15 feet = phenomenal. SCI method (16C): length of body along line of body. RW method (18): length of body peg to peg.

The Perfect Shot: Mini Edition for Africa

Crocodile

The Hunt — Extremely challenging to hunt; see, hear, and smell extremely well; also able to detect ground vibrations and have "feathered watchdogs." Absolutely precise first-shot placement essential to "anchor" a big croc successfully. Ambush known basking site. Baiting the most successful hunting method. Secure bait at water's edge. Use any form of meat as bait. Replenish daily until territorial bull has eaten his fill and lies next to bait to guard it. Build blind downwind. Shooting distance: longest range at which a golf-ball-sized target can be hit with the chosen rifle/calibre/scope combination (50–80 paces). Stable shooting rest essential (sandbags). Measure blind/bait distance carefully. Sight rifle in at this distance.

Rifle, Calibre, and Bullet Selection — Trophy-sized croc requires surgically precise first shot placement. Selection must be capable of this. The .338s or .35s and 250-grain premium-quality softpoint bullets a sensible minimum. Larger calibres, 9.3mms and .375 H&H, a better choice if sufficiently accurate. Quality expanding bullets essential. Scope also essential: 1.5–5X variable a good choice.

Shot Placement — "Anchoring" first shot requires knowledge of skull and neck. Brain golf-ball sized and lies midway between eyes and ear ridges, two inches below eye level. Side-on brain shot: Depending on angle, place shot just above the bend in the "L" of the smile. Side-on neck/spinal shot: Place shot at end of smile or in middle of neck along its length; compensate for downward shooting angle when the croc is below eye level. Full frontal shot: Place bullet on midline, slightly behind eyes. Full going-away shot: Place shot behind head, on midline. Backup shots: Place through shoulders and hips.

Crocodile

Side-on head-only anatomy diagram

Crocodile

On a fully broadside hyena, come up the centre of the foreleg and place a high heart/lung shot on that line at the height of the shoulder joint. Place a high shoulder/spinal shot higher and farther forward on the shoulder as indicated.

Hyena

SPOTTED HYENA
Crocuta crocuta

Natural History — Strange-looking, doglike creatures; considered vermin for many years. Spotted hyena most common species; striped hyena (*Hyaena hyaena*) and brown hyena (*Hyaena brunnea*) also found locally. Scavengers but also efficient and cunning predators. Giggle and whoop—the sounds of Africa. Will eat almost anything. Raid camps. Can be a real nuisance. Mainly active at night, but will scavenge and feed during daylight when the opportunity arises. Weigh 100 to 190 pounds. Tall, powerful shoulders, muscular neck, weak and sloping hindquarters. Social animals, living in family groups or clans. Females dominant; bigger and heavier than males.

Sex Determination — Very difficult. No sex specified on the hunting permit or license because of this. Originally thought to be hermaphrodites. Only way to determine sex is to compare body size if more than one animal present. Females bigger than males.

Trophy Assessment — SCI method (15): combined length and greatest width of skull in inches. Not ranked in RW.

The Hunt — Can be a real challenge. Hyena are primarily nocturnal. Shy and elusive. Can be very cautious/elusive when hunted regularly. Hunting at night or by torchlight illegal in most African countries. Only way to hunt hyena successfully during legal shooting hours is to bait them. Build a blind and be in it at least an hour before sunset or first shooting light. Use any large animal carcass for bait. Secure just out of reach so hyena "hang around."

Rifle, Calibre, and Bullet Selection — Any rifle/calibre/scope combination suitable for the majority of Africa's medium-sized antelope species will do—the various 7mms or .30 calibres and conventional softpoint bullets. A good scope with a well-defined or illuminated reticle is essential for the low-light conditions in which most shots at hyena will be taken.

Shot Placement — Side-on high heart/lung most effective: Sight up the front leg and place shot squarely on body's horizontal midline. High shoulder/spinal shot: Shoot farther forward and higher up the shoulder, through centre of shoulder blade; should drop to the shot. Frontal shots: Place bullet squarely into centre of chest, at base of neck between shoulder joints. Quartering shots: Be sure to get angles right so bullet either stays in or passes through chest cavity. Head shots: Avoid if skull is to be measured for record-book purposes.

Anatomy diagram

Hyena

Giraffe

From the side, the heart is positioned well forward, in the very front of the chest. Here the aiming points for the high heart/lung, high shoulder/spinal, and neck/spinal shots are indicated.

GIRAFFE
Giraffa camelopardalis

Natural History — Translation of *camelopardalis* is body size and shape of a camel and the spots of a leopard. Tallest and heaviest of the world's hoofed animals. Mature bulls stand as tall as nineteen feet; an average giraffe can weigh 1½ tons. Two short, skin-covered, callous-tipped, bony "horns" on top of head. "Horns" larger and better developed in mature males. Subspecies differ in hide color, pattern, and "horn" development. Predominantly browsers. Feed mainly during daylight hours. Never lie flat on the ground, rarely sleep. Very keen eyesight. Docile by nature but will defend themselves when attacked, using front feet. Man and lion their only predators. Loosely associated herd structure.

Sex Determination — Mature giraffe bulls are considerably larger and almost twice as heavy as even the biggest of cows. Also considerably darker in overall color. Mature bulls are usually solitary; emit an offensive, musty odor (known as "stink bulls"); have bigger, better-developed "horns" and a median horn in the middle of the forehead. Penis sheath clearly visible on the bottom of the belly line. Mature cows rarely encountered alone.

Trophy Assessment — Not recorded in any of the record books but can make a most unusual trophy.

The Hunt — Giraffe have exceptionally keen eyesight, acute hearing, and cautious dispositions. The terrain in which they are found can make approaching them a real challenge. Great wanderers; can cover large distances each day. Neither water dependent nor territorial. Cloven-hoofed feet and considerable body weight create distinctive spoor. Hunt by either spot and stalk or track, walk, and stalk.

Rifle, Calibre, and Bullet Selection — Giraffe have thick, tough skin; require same bullet selection as for a pachyderm. Although the hotter 7mms are legal, the 9.3mms or .375 H&H and quality solids are the minimum calibres recommended for all body shots. Larger calibres even more effective. Premium-quality expanding bullets more effective for spinal and brain shots. Solids for body shots.

Shot Placement — Brain surprisingly small; positioned beneath and between the two "horns." Heart lies in centre of chest cavity, far forward, midway between and extending above shoulder joints (two prominent bumps on front edge of chest). Lungs also positioned well forward and high up in chest cavity. They are V-shaped with only a small portion extending behind the heart. Heart/lung shot: Place shot on centre line of foreleg, above shoulder "bumps." Brain shot: Place shot between ear and eye, below "horns." Remember to compensate for upward shooting angle. Low neck/spinal shot: Place shot in centre of neck, where it joins body. High neck/spinal shot: Place through centre of neck where it joins head. Frontal chest shot: Shoot between and slightly above prominent shoulder joints, or somewhat higher for spine at base of neck. Quartering frontal shots: Aim to break the prominent shoulder joint. Quartering-away shots: Take only as a last resort; heart and lungs are situated high up in chest cavity.

Anatomy diagram

Giraffe

Eland

A mature eland bull's massive, deep chest and prominent dewlap often cause hunters to place the shot too high. The aiming point for a high heart/lung shot is indicated.

ELAND

Taurotragus oryx (common), *Taurotragus derbianus* (giant)

Natural History — Two species of eland—the common and the giant. Largest of Africa's horned antelope species. Can outweigh a mature buffalo. Not territorial; great wanderers. Extremely wary, alert, and cautious. Impressive jumpers; man-made barriers no obstacle. Mixed feeders, browse more than graze, require a high-protein diet. Drink when water is freely available but can survive on the moisture they obtain from their diet. Gregarious herd animals. Herds occasionally number in the hundreds. Up to three subspecies of common eland and two subspecies of giant eland recognized.

Sex Determination — Both sexes carry spiral, ridged horns, but those of mature bulls are thicker and more massive (particularly at the bases). Bull horns V-shaped; cow horns more parallel and vertical. Trophy eland called "blue bulls"; name derived from blue color that develops with advanced age in neck, head, and shoulder areas. Bulls larger, better muscled, and generally more massive than cows, with well-developed, square-edged dewlap at bottom edge of neck. Forehead usually covered with thick mat of hair.

Trophy Assessment — Horns of the giant species considerably thicker, longer, and more impressive looking. SCI method (2): length of both horns around spiral ridge + circumference of both horns at bases. RW method (8): length of longest horn.

The Hunt — Easy way: chance encounter, while out hunting some other game species. Pursuit of trophy bulls difficult. Find suitable spoor and track, walk, and stalk. Alert and wary species, difficult to approach to within shooting distance. Bulls most often shot in relatively thick cover at close range.

Rifle, Calibre, and Bullet Selection — Quick-pointing double rifle in either O/U or S/S configuration, in 9.3x74R calibre with either 293-grain TUG bullets by RWS or 286-grain solids and topped off with a good German 1.5–5X scope a good choice for "thick bush" situations. Alternatively, the .375 H&H and good-quality expanding bullets or the 9.3x62mm and 286-grain Barnes X bullets would be good choices. Hot 7mms legal minimum but are considered by many PHs to be "too small" for eland.

Shot Placement — Side-on, top-of-the-heart/lung shot: Place on centre line of front leg, no higher than midway up body. Neck/spinal shot: Place just in front of shoulder fractionally below midline. Shoulder/spinal shot: Place higher up on shoulder, through scapula. Quartering frontal shots: Place bullet to hit shoulder joint. Quartering-away shots: Place bullet to exit through gap between front legs. Going-away, "Texas heart shot" ("backing" shots only; use solids): Place squarely into the centre of behind, right at anus.

The Perfect Shot: Mini Edition for Africa

Side-on anatomy diagram

The aiming points for the high heart/lung, the high shoulder/spinal, and the neck/spinal shots from the fully broadside position are marked.

Greater Kudu

GREATER KUDU
Tragelaphus strepsiceros

Natural History — Majestic, strikingly beautiful, striped, spiral-horned antelope. Relatively large and heavy but perfectly camouflaged coloring; nicknamed "Gray Ghosts of Africa." Sly, secretive, elusive; exceptional senses. Cows give a warning bark when danger is sensed. Almost exclusively browsers. Graze only occasionally. Preferred habitat is rocky, hilly, or mountainous areas, interspersed with woodland or thick bush. Drink regularly; never far from water, but can be encountered in some extremely arid areas. Highly adaptable, excellent jumpers, fully capable of clearing a seven-foot fence. Gregarious herd animals. Great wanderers. Life expectancy 12 to 13 years. Up to five subspecies recognized.

Sex Determination — Only kudu bulls carry horns. A rare horned female may be encountered, but horns are usually small stubs or buttons. Females tan/brown, bulls usually dark gray.

Trophy Assessment — Field estimation extremely difficult; depth of curl varies. Large curl, better score. Base circumferences of a good set of horns should measure between 10½ and 12 inches each. SCI method (2): length of both horns around spiral ridge + circumference of both horns at bases. RW method (8): length of longest horn. Horn length in the low 50s fairly common; 55+ really good trophies; 60+ exceptional.

The Hunt — Several hunting methods for kudu: Glass likely feeding spots early in the morning, assess the terrain, and stalk.   Ambush a known feeding field in an agricultural area at first light or as they return to high ground. Kudu are regular drinkers; ambush them on the move either to or from a water hole, usually at midday. Can be tracked in sandy areas. Still-hunting through thick cover also successful.

Rifle, Calibre, and Bullet Selection — The .270 Win., 7x57mm, .308 Win., and .30-06, with controlled-expansion softpoint bullets in 150-, 175-, 180-, and 220-grain weights, respectively, are as small a calibre and light a bullet recommended. Good scope essential for longer shots.

Shot Placement — Neck or head shot can ruin a shoulder mount. High heart/lung shot most recommended: Place shot through centre of vital triangle (triangle formed by shoulder blade, point of shoulder, and elbow joint). High shoulder/spinal shot: Place shot squarely through centre of scapula. Lung shot recommended for the biltong hunter: Place just behind shoulder. Quartering-on shots: Place on or just inside shoulder joint. Going-away shots difficult as kudu are narrow, slab-sided antelope; consider only as last resort.

Greater Kudu

A young stallion fully broadside, the best position from which to take either a high heart/lung or a shoulder/spinal shot.

Zebra

ZEBRA
Equus spp.

Natural History — Sport hunted for their skin and as source of bait for both lion and leopard. Can weigh over 700 pounds. Extremely efficient grazers, always fat. Water-dependent; never too far from water even though they can occur in extremely arid areas. Gregarious herd animals, most often encountered in small family units. Slow-maturing and long-lived animals. Stallions obnoxious creatures—always kicking, biting, and fighting among themselves.

Sex Determination — Very difficult; reason why most hunting permits do not specify the sex to be taken. Stallions and mares have similar pattern configurations and similar body size and weight. Stallion neck thicker, head larger compared to overall body size. Behavior in the herd important: When spooked, a family group will always be led away by mare; stallion follows at the rear and often stops to look back. Whenever a herd approaches water, stallion will lead. When the herd is feeding peacefully or resting, the stallion will usually be on the periphery. More brown between stripes of stallion.

Trophy Assessment — For trophies, old stallions usually have scarred/damaged, lower-quality hides; young bachelor-herd stallions have the best skins, a fact that makes them the targets of choice. For baiting purposes, any stallion or old, barren mare will do.

Zebra

The Hunt — Zebra most active during the early morning and late afternoon. Non-territorial but have home ranges. Frequent and regular drinkers; prefer clean, clear water; rarely venture far from this source. Usually drink at night. Donkey-like spoor distinctive and easy to follow. Find fresh spoor at a water source and follow it, or glass all likely areas of suitable habitat. In mountainous areas, glass from elevated point at first light.

Rifle, Calibre, and Bullet Selection — Zebra require a minimum calibre/bullet combination in the .270, 7mm, or .30-calibre range and controlled-expansion softpoint bullets of at least 150 grains in weight. They also require precise shot placement.

Shot Placement — High heart/lung shot most recommended: Sight up centre line of front leg and place shot on that line somewhere between one-third and halfway up body. High shoulder/spinal shot: Place shot higher up and farther forward on shoulder, through centre of shoulder blade. Spine shot: Place shot in middle of neck where it joins body. Frontal chest shot: Place full frontal shot squarely into its centre, at base of neck.

Zebra

Zebra

Even with the bull's right leg in the rearward position, the top of the heart is still in the centre of the vital triangle. The aiming point for a high heart/lung shot is marked.

SABLE
Hippotragus niger

Natural History — Impressive and sought-after trophy animal. Distinctive white facial and belly markings; black coat. Heavily ridged, backward-sweeping horns. Aggressive; will not hesitate to charge if wounded, cornered, or simply threatened. Gregarious herd animals. Master bull dominates a herd, but oldest and wisest cow leads it. Frequent drinkers; territory near permanent source of water. Selective grazing animals. Three subspecies are recognized.

Sex Determination — Both sexes carry horns, but those of trophy bulls are considerably thicker, more heavily ridged, and sweepingly curved. Mature bulls are pitch-black, with a distinctly white underbelly. Cows darken with age but retain a dull rusty red tinge; have thinner, straighter horns.

Trophy Assessment — Trophy quality properly assessed only from the side-on position. Horn length of 40 inches or more considered good for common sable. Horns on giant sable can reach nearly 60 inches in length. SCI method (1): length of both horns + circumference of both horns at bases. RW method (7): length of longest horn.

The Hunt — Most active during the early morning and late afternoon; like to graze in or near open grasslands. Water-dependent species; encountered in areas of suitable habitat near water. Look for arrowhead-shaped spoor in the vicinity of watering points. Catch sable at first light while they are still out feeding in an open, short-grass, or recently burned-off area. Herd bull will usually be somewhere on the periphery. Proud and aloof antelope; not all that difficult to approach.

Rifle, Calibre, and Bullet Selection — Sable are heavy, tough, and potentially aggressive antelope. Do not be undergunned. Legal minimum is .270 Win., but the .30-06 or .300 H&H and 200- or 220-grain controlled-expansion softpoints are a more sensible option. An even better choice is .338s and 250-grain bullets, as are the 9.3mms or .375 H&H.

Shot Placement — Be careful not to damage trophy or cape. Side-on high heart/lung shot most recommended because of this: Place shot through centre of "vital triangle." High shoulder shot from the side-on position: Place shot through centre of shoulder blade. Neck/spinal shot: Place shot through centre of neck where it joins body. Full frontal shot: Place shot squarely into centre of chest at shoulder-joint level.

Side-on anatomy picture

The site for a high heart/lung shot is marked.

Waterbuck

WATERBUCK
Kobus ellipsiprymnus

Natural History — Terrible to eat but stately to look at. High water requirement; regular and frequent drinkers; usually encountered near some form of water. Oily skin. White markings on rump (defassa group have solid white rump patch; ringed or common group have large white ring). Gregarious herd animals. Life expectancy is up to fifteen years. Predominantly grazers. Up to six waterbuck subspecies recognized.

Sex Determination — Only waterbuck bulls have horns. The horns of a really good trophy bull are large, impressive, and easy to identify.

Trophy Assessment — Horns can be properly assessed only from the front; length, degree of divergence, and thickness of bases are all easy to see and evaluate from this angle. Look for bulls with the high-scoring combination of good horn length and horn symmetry and thick, heavy bases. SCI method (1): length of both horns + circumference of both horns at bases. RW method (7): length of longest horn. Good head is 29 inches, 30 inches is very good, anything over 31 inches is superb.

The Hunt — Bulls territorial. Like open grasslands and flood plains near large stretches of water. Have good eyesight and hearing. Good binocular essential. Not all that difficult to approach. Can also be encountered in thickly bushed areas.

Rifle, Calibre, and Bullet Selection — Trophy waterbuck weigh 550 to 600 pounds. For open grassland conditions, the .270 Win. and quality 150-grain softpoint bullets are as small a calibre and as light a bullet recommended; the various 7mms and .30 calibres with good 175- to 220-grain controlled-expansion softpoints a better, more effective option, especially for "bush" areas.

Shot Placement — Shoulder mount best way to display waterbuck. Avoid neck shots, which could ruin cape. High heart/lung shot recommended: Sight up the front leg and place the shot on that line somewhere between one-third and halfway up the body. Shoulder/spinal shot: Place higher up on shoulder, above body's horizontal midline and somewhat farther forward, through middle of the shoulder blade. Full frontal: Place shot squarely into centre of chest at base of neck.

The Perfect Shot: Mini Edition for Africa

Side-on anatomy diagram

Waterbuck

There is a tendency to shoot high on broadside wildebeest. From this angle, never place a shot above the body's horizontal midline. Both the high heart/lung and the shoulder/spinal shot placement sites are marked.

Wildebeest

WILDEBEEST

Connochaetes gnou (black), *Connochaetes taurinus* (brindled)

Natural History — Direct translation of wildebeest means "wild ox," but it is a member of the antelope family. Two varieties: *Connochaetes gnou*, black wildebeest, and *Connochaetes taurinus*, common or brindled wildebeest. Black wildebeest relatively rare. Brindled wildebeest has head of a moose; beard of a goat; hump, neck, and shoulders of an ox; hindquarters of an antelope; and mane and tail of a horse. Gregarious herd animals; herds may be many thousands when migrating. Exclusively short-grass grazers. Up to four subspecies of *Connochaetes taurinus* recognized.

Sex Determination — Not easy to distinguish. Both sexes have horns and are similar in body size and color. Breeding bulls deeper bodied, more masculine looking. Old bulls darker with more and wider stripes on their sides. Forehead and muzzle pitch black, no trace of brown. Horn bases thick and well developed; horns may droop slightly to just below level of the extended ear tips before curling upward. During rut, tree bark stain appears on horns near bases.

Trophy Assessment — Properly assessed only from the front. Look for big, easily visible bosses and a horn spread greater than width of the extended ear tips. Important to assess trophy bull's mane and beard for shoulder mount. SCI method (5) for common wildebeest: tip-to-tip measurement of horns + circumference of bosses of both horns. RW method (12) for common wildebeest: outside spread + inside spread + length of longest horn + width of wider boss. For measurement methods for black wildebeest, see Appendix III.

The Hunt — On plains and dry, open spaces, wildebeest easy to locate from a distance. In bushveld conditions, more difficult; can be elusive and shy. In sandy, sparsely grassed areas, can be hunted by tracking (splayed toes, deeply imprinted forefeet spoor). Productive hunting method is to walk slowly through likely resting areas, into or across the wind. Stop frequently and glass well ahead; look for movement.

Rifle, Calibre, and Bullet Selection — Wildebeest are remarkably tough antelope. For open terrain hunting, the .270 Win. and good 150-grain bullets minimum recommendation; 7mm Rem. Mag. with 160- or 175-grain bullets, .300 H&H and .300 Win. Mag. with 200- or 220-grain bullets better options. Even larger calibres recommended for "bushveld" conditions.

Shot Placement — Prominent hump on shoulders and mane can lead to body shots being placed too high. Side-on, high heart/lung shot recommended: Come up back edge of front leg and place shot a hand's width above the point of the elbow. Side-on, spinal shot: Aim for front edge of shoulder, exactly in middle of neck where it joins body. Full frontal chest shot from low down position: Place squarely into centre of chest, just below shoulder joints. Full frontal brain shot: Place shot in centre of forehead, just above eye level and in line with base of ears.

Side-on anatomy diagram

Wildebeest

The deep chest and neck of the gemsbok can complicate shot placement. Both the high heart/lung and shoulder/spinal shots are indicated. (Photo by SATOUR)

Oryx/Gemsbok

ORYX / GEMSBOK
Oryx gazella

Natural History — Known as the "desert warrior." Courageous; extremely aggressive and dangerous when cornered, injured, or threatened. Primarily an open-country species. Survive and thrive in hot, waterless expanses. Can survive without surface drinking water for many months. Grazers; will also browse if necessary. Gregarious herd animals. Four subspecies of *Oryx gazella* recognized. *Oryx dammah*, the scimitar-horned oryx, occurs on the southern edge of the Sahara.

Sex Determination — Both sexes carry horns. Mature females slightly smaller in overall size; horns of mature females usually longer and considerably slimmer, bases less massive, horns may curve rearward slightly. Bull horns thicker, straighter.

Trophy Assessment — Trophies of either sex are eligible for record-book entry. Females may outscore males because of greater horn length. SCI method (1): length of both horns + circumference of both horns at bases. RW method (7): length of longest horn.

The Hunt — Have to cover great distances, catch up with herd, get close enough for shot. Needed: good pair of boots, suitably powered binocular, and relatively flat-shooting rifle/calibre combination. Gemsbok extremely

Oryx/Gemsbok

alert with remarkably good eyesight, hearing, and smell. Sex determination and trophy assessment are difficult, thus adding greatly to the challenge. Provide very fine eating.

Calibre, Rifle, and Bullet Selection — For wide-open spaces, 6X-scoped flat-shooters and the right type, shape, and weight of bullet to complement suitable calibres are absolutely essential. Minimum recommendation: .270 Win. and 150-grain controlled-expansion softpoints. Hot 7mms and .30mms better. For bushveld conditions, heavy-for-calibre, round-nose, bush-busting bullets at modest velocity best. 7mm Mauser and good 175-grain softpoints minimum recommendation.

Shot Placement — Tendency to shoot too high; never shoot above horizontal midline. Broadside high heart/lung shot: Come up back edge of front leg to spot about a third of the way up body and no higher than midline. Side-on neck shot: Place just in front of shoulder and fractionally below midline.

Anatomy diagram

Oryx/Gemsbok

A red hartebeest bull broadside. Notice his thick horn bases. Place a high heart/lung shot as indicated.

HARTEBEEST
Alcelaphus spp.

Natural History — Hartebeest (*Alcelaphus* spp.) are cousins of the topi, tsessebe, bontebok, and blesbok (*Damaliscus* spp.). Long, narrow heads, yellow goat-like eyes, slender necks, long, pointed ears, prominently high withers, a sloping backline, matchstick legs, and relatively unimpressive horns. Very fleet with legendary endurance. Horns originate at the very top of the head from a pedicel. Not particularly difficult to hunt; meat quality considered poor. Good for camp rations and bait. Gregarious herd animals. Primarily grazers; prefer open grasslands, *vlei* areas, and semidesert bush savanna. Feed during cooler times of day. Drink when water available but can go without. Up to nine subspecies of *A. buselaphus* recognized. Northern or bubal hartebeest is extinct. Same genus but different species: *A. lichtensteini*, Lichtenstein hartebeest.

Sex Determination — Mature males more robustly built, generally darker in color. Both male and female carry heavily ringed horns. Horn size and shape vary according to the particular subspecies, but with shape similar between the sexes of a subspecies. Horn bases of mature bulls considerably thicker and more massive than those of females.

Trophy Evaluation — Essential to evaluate from both the frontal and side-on positions. SCI method (1): length of both horns + circumference of both horns at bases. RW method (7): length of longest horn.

The Hunt — Easy to locate in open-country areas. Glass from an elevated vantage point; also check salt pans and mineral licks. Ambush herd arriving at or leaving shady resting place. Good hearing, acute sense of smell; eyesight not all that good. Vulnerable to stalk at first or last light.

Rifle, Calibre, and Bullet Selection — Relatively flat-shooting calibre necessary as shots are usually longish. The .270 Win. and quality 130-grain expanding bullets a sensible minimum. The various 7mms and 140-grain bullets of good ballistic coefficient probably better. The .308 Win. and .30-06 with bullets in the 165-grain weight range also suitable if sighted in appropriately.

Shot Placement — Humped withers often cause hunters to shoot too high. Side-on high heart/lung shot recommended: Place no higher than body's midline, along line of back edge of front leg. Shoulder/spinal shot: Place slightly higher up and farther forward on the shoulder itself. Neck/spinal shot: Necks usually too slender for this shot to be recommended. Frontal shot: Place between the shoulder joints only if the head is lifted up high or turned to the side.

Impala

The graceful impala is one of Africa's most popular medium-sized antelope. This southern ram will make the book with ease. The placement sites for both the neck/spinal and high shoulder/spinal shots are marked.

IMPALA
Aepyceros melampus

Natural History — "Bread and butter" antelope. Commonly used as camp meat and as bait for leopard; good for "cutting hunting teeth." Lyre-shaped horns; two oval, raised, black-haired scent glands located on the inside of their hind legs just above the hoof. Gregarious herd animals. Both graze and browse; prefer open, heavily grazed, almost barren areas adjacent to or within open woodland, bushveld, or mopane scrub. Never venture far from water; must drink at least once daily. Three subspecies recognized

Sex Determination — Only rams have horns, but propensity to clump together in thick bush makes it difficult to tell the difference.

Trophy Assessment — Look for horns with long, smooth, and sharply pointed tips, also for tips that point vertically and are parallel with each other or diverge outward. SCI method (1): length of both horns + circumference of both horns at bases. RW method (7): length of longest horn.

The Hunt — During autumn rut and wintertime hunting season, best rams are usually found with breeding herds. Have superb eyesight, hearing, and sense of smell. Most active during the cooler times of the day. Ambush known feeding areas. When alarmed, impala will bunch together, making it easy to accidentally shoot more than one with a single shot.

The Perfect Shot: Mini Edition for Africa

Rifle, Calibre, and Bullet Selection — Although the .22 centrefires are legal, they are not recommended. The 6mms (.243 Win.) are much more effective. The 7x57mm with 175-grain roundnose softpoints has a wonderful reputation for bushveld conditions. The .308 Win., .30-06, and 180-grain softs also a good choice. 4X scope most useful.

Shot Placement — Tough for their size. High heart/lung shot recommended: Place into centre of "vital triangle." High lung shot spoils less "good eating" meat: Place just behind shoulder from the side-on position, directly above elbow, where fawn-colored part of hide changes to a rusty brick brownish orange. Neck shot: Place into centre of neck anywhere along its length. Brain shots: Only for the experienced hunter; this shot is the domain of the professional "culler" and not the sport or meat hunter.

Impala

Side-on anatomy diagram

C. ROBERTSON ©

A good Chobe ram. A high heart/ lung shot would be the safest and surest in this situation. (Photo by S. Watlon)

Bushbuck

BUSHBUCK
Tragelaphus scriptus

Natural History — Challenging to hunt, shy and elusive. Weigh 80 to 140 pounds. Subspecies vary widely in color, pattern, and extent of stripes, chevrons, blazes, and dots. Body and horn size can also vary considerably. Solitary animals; trophy bucks encountered as loners. Have distinct home ranges. Almost exclusively browsers. Life expectancy about 12 years. Alarm signal is a dog-like bark. Up to nine subspecies recognized.

Sex Determination — Only male bushbuck carry horns. Mature bucks are considerably larger and stockier than females of the species, generally darker overall. Females light brown to fawn; males chestnut brown to almost black.

Trophy Assessment — Relatively easy to assess from the front. Thickness of horns and visible length influence high trophy scores. Horn tips usually point upward, parallel to each other. Even better are horn tips that diverge outward. SCI method (2): length of horns around spiral ridge + circumference of both horns at bases. RW method (8): length of longest horn measured around spiral.

The Hunt — Often likened to hunting the American white-tailed deer. Look for suitable habitat, areas of thick vegetation bordering rivers. Still-hunting through suitable habitat is one of the most productive hunting methods. Walk into or across the wind, moving quietly, stopping frequently to probe the densest cover. Wounded bushbuck are aggressive, will not hesitate to charge.

Rifle, Calibre, and Bullet Selection — The 7x57mm, .308 Win., or .30-06 and suitable 175-, 180-, and 220-grain bullets are sensible minimums for bushbuck.

Shot Placement — Care should be taken to avoid damaging either cape or horns. This rules out brain shot and neck/spinal shot. From any angle, place shot so that bullet gets into or passes through chest cavity; this should not be difficult with calibre/bullet combinations recommended.

The Perfect Shot: Mini Edition for Africa

Bushbuck

Springbok

The horns of trophy-quality springbok rams such as this have angled curves and thick bases. In really good specimens, horn length is twice that of the erect ears. The high heart/lung and neck/spinal shots are indicated. (Photo by SATOUR)

SPRINGBOK
Antidorcas marsupialis

Natural History — National emblem of South Africa; name means "jump buck," for their *stotting*, a pogo-stick style of jumping when alarmed. Exclusively a southern African species. Weight varies by subspecies; mature males 75 to 100 pounds. Gregarious herd animals of dry, open grassland and semi-desert. Both grazers and browsers, preferring short-grass terrain with stunted semi-desert shrubs and bushes. Not dependent on water but will drink daily when water available. Up to three subspecies and two color phases recognized.

Sex Determination — Although of similar size, mature females are generally lighter in weight. Both sexes carry horns. Those of females thinner, spindlier looking, also straighter, more upright, and less curved. Tips are usually bent, pointing inward toward each other. Horns of trophy-quality rams longer, more obviously curved, considerably thicker and more massive, more conspicuously ridged. The older a male gets, the more rearward-pointing the tips will become.

Trophy Evaluation — Difficult; horns relatively small, hard to get close enough to evaluate. Base thickness and overall length important; curves more angular on good specimens. Main body of the horns splayed. Look for horn length twice that of erect ears. SCI method (1): length of both horns + circumference of both horns at bases. RW method (7): length of longest horn.

Springbok

The Hunt — Renowned as tastiest of all African antelope. Demand high among meat hunters. Harvested on game farms through rifle culling. Great challenge to hunt in the wild. Phenomenal eyesight, natural paranoia about being approached; challenging to hunt by sight-and-stalk methods. Be prepared for much walking and crawling. Ambush known feeding areas like fringes of pans or physical barriers like fence lines. Shooting distances of up to 300 paces are normal.

Rifle, Calibre, and Bullet Selection — Flat-shooters essential as shots out to 300 paces common. Often windy. Choose calibres capable of firing bullets of at least 120 grains in weight, at muzzle velocities in excess of 2,600 fps; .257 Roberts, .25-06 Rem., the various 6.5mms, the .264 Win. Mag., the .270 Win., and the various 7mms are all good choices. A 6X scope essential for such long-range shots.

Shot Placement — Side-on lung shot (just behind shoulder) shot of choice for the meat hunter. Side-on high heart/lung shot recommended for the trophy hunter. Head shots not recommended; only for the professional "culler."

Side-on anatomy diagram

Springbok

Viewed from the side, the long mane hairs may cover the top of the shoulder. The high heart/lung shot is the best option here, and it is marked.

WARTHOG
Phacochoerus aethiopicus

Natural History — Distant cousin of the European boar; popular with safari clients. Ugly to the point of being lovable. Hunted for trophy purposes, tusks, hide. Also one of the better-tasting game meats and a good bait for leopard. Can weigh as much as 250 pounds. One of the toughest of all African species. Active during daylight; spend night in unused antbear burrows. Almost exclusively grazers. Not territorial, wander wherever food supply dictates. Love to wallow in mud and take dust baths. Not entirely water dependent, but will drink regularly when water is available. Frequently encountered near wet, marshy areas. Root with their snouts. Occur in small family groups or "sounders."

Sex Determination — Warthog get name from their facial "warts." All warthog have a pair of warts; males have a second pair on the side of the muzzle just above the upper tusks. Testicles on mature boar easily visible. Mature boars are considerably larger and more massive than sows, with bigger and thicker tusks.

Trophy Assessment — Warthog have two sets of tusks, but only the larger upper-jaw pair is measured. Tusks easily visible, but one-third to as much as one-half embedded in the skull. Look for tusks with good visible thickness and length. SCI method (12): length of both tusks + circumference of both tusks at largest place. RW method (6): length of longest tusk.

The Perfect Shot: Mini Edition for Africa

The Hunt — Search for suitable feeding grounds (pans, marshy areas, recently burned-off *vleis*). They feed throughout the day. Their eyes are close to the ground, so they do not see well; however, they have excellent hearing and a good sense of smell. Approach slowly from downwind. Ambush a mud wallow or feeding area.

Rifle, Calibre, and Bullet Selection — The various 7mms and the .30 calibres with quality 160- to 180-grain softpoint bullets are a good choice. On big, trophy-sized hogs, larger calibres are more effective.

Shot Placement — The barrel roundness of a big trophy hog, long mane hairs, and apparent absence of a neck can make shot placement challenging. Side-on, high heart/lung shot most effective: Sight up centre line of front leg and shoot when point of aim is just below body's midline. Side-on brain shot: Place shot just in front of ear's base. Frontal brain shot common, as warthog are inquisitive: Place between eyes. Rear-end or "Texas heart shot": Place shot just below anus.

Anatomy diagram

ROBERTSON ©

Duiker

This is a young southern bush duiker male. Notice his long, pointed ears and the tuft of hair on the very top of his head, between the horns. The best shot placement for a relatively fast and fragile bullet is marked. (Photo by C. Nel)

DUIKER
Subfamily *Cephalophinae*

Natural History — Name derived from the Dutch *duik,* meaning "to dive," and describes their low scooting type of running. The species vary greatly in weight, from less than 9 to more than 175 pounds. Bush duikers need bush for browse and protection, giving rise to their common name. Forest duikers (genus *Cephalophus*) found in wet, lush forest. Solitary antelope, most often encountered alone. Fertile and prolific breeders. Most active during the late afternoon and early evening, but become nocturnal when subjected to intensive hunting pressure. Extremely varied diet; primarily browsers, but will feed on other foodstuffs not usually considered antelope food. Able to survive in proximity to man. Not dependent on water; get sufficient moisture from their varied diet. Four subspecies of bush duiker and up to twenty species of forest duiker recognized.

Sex Determination — Bush duikers: Only males carry horns. A few horned females, but horns small. Mature females somewhat larger than even the biggest males. Forest duikers: Both sexes are horned. Females slightly bigger in body size, usually encountered only as individuals.

Trophy Evaluation — Estimating horn length: When a trophy specimen bush duiker looks at you with its long and pointed ears cocked, horn tips level with the ear points are roughly four inches long. High-scoring trophies are those with horn tips that extend an inch or more above the level of the cocked ear points. Forest duiker horns vary greatly by species from just over an inch to over seven inches for trophy specimens. SCI method (1A): length of both horns + circumference of both horns at bases. RW method (7): length of longest horn.

The Hunt — Difficult to hunt; super-refined senses, small size, neutral coloring, habit of staying in or close to long grass or thick bush. Commonly hunted with shotguns; usually taken as short-range running targets as they break cover or when driven by beaters. Many taken in chance encounters during hunts for something bigger. Still-hunting through known duiker habitat or ambushing a likely feeding area at first light also effective. Calling is the most productive method for the forest duikers.

Rifle, Calibre, and Bullet Selection — Virtually all the hunting calibres—from the 6mm and 100-grain bullets all the way up to the ubiquitous .375 H&H and 300-grain softpoints—have been used with success on these diminutive antelope. Good scope essential for the tricky light conditions under which many trophy duiker are taken. Shooting distances are usually short; 4X is enough.

Shot Placement — Side-on high heart/lung shot: Place on line of foreleg, just below body's midline; quick-expanding bullet will make finding trophy easier. High shoulder/spinal shot: Place shot high up and well forward on shoulder, through centre of shoulder blade; duiker should drop to the shot, therefore be easy to find.

Anatomy diagram

From the side, be sure to place a shot well behind the shoulders if using a conventional lead-core softpoint bullet.

Klipspringer

KLIPSPRINGER

Oreotragus oreotragus

Natural History — "Ballerina of the rocks." Name means "rock jumper." Amazing agility to jump from rock to rock and effortlessly race up sheer cliff faces. Body covered with dense layer of short, quill-like hairs. Important member of Africa's "small five" (with the bush duiker, grysbok, steenbok, and oribi). Highly sought-after trophy, exceedingly good eating, excellent bait for attracting leopard. Occur in many of the continent's more arid and rugged mountain ranges. Incredible agility and balance. Predominantly browsers. Well suited to dry, harsh environment, but drink when water is available. Most commonly encountered as individuals, in male/female pairs, or as small family groups. Most active during the cooler daylight hours. Alarm call is a loud, shrill whistle.

Sex Determination — Only males carry horns. Females tend to be slightly bigger and a little heavier.

Trophy Evaluation — Horns can be seen through binocular even from a distance. Compare horn length to that of the erect ears: Horns just above ear tips should be around 4 inches. SCI measurement (1A): length of both horns + circumference of both horns at bases. RW method (7): length of longest horn.

The Hunt — Look for suitably rocky terrain or mountain ranges. Hunt from bottom looking upward (they are used to predation from above). Shrill alarm whistle often gives their presence away. Habit of stopping to look

The Perfect Shot: Mini Edition for Africa

back down at intruders provides shooting opportunity. Climb slowly after them; they usually don't go far and prefer to keep their tormentor in sight.

Rifle, Calibre, and Bullet Selection — Requires only a .22 centrefire and a decently constructed 45- to 55-grain bullet, but is usually hunted with heavier calibres. Larger calibres and overly fragile bullets can ruin the cape. Solids in .22 calibre, even ex-military-issue FMJ ammo for the .223, are a good idea. A good scope and a quality binocular are essential for precise shot placement and trophy evaluation from a distance.

Shot Placement — Important when shooting with a softpoint bullet to hit a klipspringer well behind the shoulder. When using solids, place side-on shots farther forward, into the rear portion of the chest cavity, but should any angles be involved, keep well clear of the shoulder and front leg bones. Shoulder/spinal or neck/spinal shot not recommended. Full frontal shots usually taken at an upward angle: Place shot low down in chest area, on brisket or even between front legs.

Klipspringer

Appendix I: Minimum requirements for inclusion in record book, number one record measurement and measurement system used, Safari Club International (SCI) and Roland Ward (RW). (Both SCI and RW use inches and pounds; see end of chart for conversion information.)

Animal	SCI			RW		
	Minimum	Record	Method	Minimum	Record	Method
Lion	23	$28^{1}/_{16}$	15	24	$28^{3}/_{4}$	17
Leopard	14	$19^{11}/_{16}$	15	$15^{3}/_{8}$	19	17
Hyena, spotted	15	$19^{14}/_{16}$	15	NC	NC	NC
Elephant	100	302	14	80	226	16
Rhino, black	56	$89^{2}/_{8}$	8	24	$53^{1}/_{2}$	15
Rhino, southern white	70	$102^{6}/_{8}$	8	28	$62^{1}/_{4}$	15
Rhino, northern white	ED	$67^{1}/_{8}$	8	28	$50^{1}/_{8}$	15
Buffalo, Cape/southern	100	141	4	42	64	12
Buffalo, Nile	80	$115^{3}/_{8}$	4	38	$44^{1}/_{4}$	12
Buffalo, C. African savanna	65	$96^{3}/_{8}$	4	NC	NC	NC
Buffalo, W. African savanna	55	81	4	37	$46^{1}/_{8}$	12
Buffalo, dwarf forest	40	$68^{5}/_{8}$	4	20	$29^{7}/_{8}$	11
Eland, Central African giant	98	$141^{3}/_{8}$	2	$44^{7}/_{8}$	$56^{1}/_{4}$	8

ED=editor's discretion; NC=no category, NE-no entry.

The Perfect Shot: Mini Edition for Africa

Animal	SCI			RW		
	Minimum	Record	Method	Minimum	Record	Method
Eland, western giant	ED	NE	2	$37^3/_4$	NE	8
Eland, Cape	77	$113^2/_8$	2	NC	NC	NC
Eland, Livingstone	79	119	2	35	$46^5/_8$	8
Eland, East African	74	$111^3/_8$	2	33	$42^1/_8$	8
Kudu, southern greater	121	$155^3/_8$	2	$53^7/_8$	$73^7/_8$	8
Kudu, Eastern Cape greater	98	$141^5/_8$	2	NC	NC	NC
Kudu, East African greater	109	$145^6/_8$	2	52	$59^7/_8$	8
Kudu, Abyssinian greater	98	$136^3/_8$	2	$42^7/_8$	$50^1/_8$	8
Kudu, western greater	ED	$120^4/_8$	2	NC	NC	NC
Bushbuck, harnessed	25	$39^4/_8$	2	$11^3/_4$	$16^1/_8$	8
Bushbuck, Nile	29	$45^6/_8$	2	$13^3/_8$	$18^3/_4$	8
Bushbuck, Abyssinian	25	$40^6/_8$	2	$13^3/_8$	NE	8
Bushbuck, Menelik or Arusi	29	$43^5/_8$	2	$11^3/_8$	$15^5/_8$	8
Bushbuck, Shoan	NC	NC	NC	$11^1/_4$	$14^5/_8$	8
Bushbuck, East African	35	53	2	16	$19^1/_4$	8
Bushbuck, Chobe	33	$52^3/_8$	2	14	$18^1/_4$	8

ED=editor's discretion; NC=no category; NE=no entry.

The Perfect Shot: Mini Edition for Africa

Animal	SCI			RW		
	Minimum	Record	Method	Minimum	Record	Method
Bushbuck, Limpopo	33	$51^{6}/_{8}$	2	15	$20^{1}/_{4}$	8
Bushbuck, Cape	31	$52^{1}/_{8}$	2	NC	NC	NC
Sable, giant or royal	ED	$141^{7}/_{8}$	1	$55^{7}/_{8}$	$64^{7}/_{8}$	7
Sable, common or typical	100	$121^{3}/_{8}$	1	$41^{7}/_{8}$	$55^{3}/_{8}$	7
Sable, Roosevelt	ED	$110^{4}/_{8}$	1	$33^{7}/_{8}$	$44^{3}/_{4}$	7
Gemsbok, Kalahari	88	$111^{5}/_{8}$	1	40	$49^{1}/_{4}$	7
Gemsbok, Angolan	78	$94^{2}/_{8}$	1	$35^{3}/_{8}$	$43^{5}/_{8}$	7
Oryx, beisa	70	$92^{7}/_{8}$	1	$30^{7}/_{8}$	43	7
Oryx, fringe-eared	68	$87^{5}/_{8}$	1	$30^{7}/_{8}$	$43^{3}/_{8}$	7
Oryx, scimitar-horned	ED	105	1	38	$50^{1}/_{8}$	7
Waterbuck, common/ringed	70	$90^{3}/_{8}$	1	28	$39^{1}/_{4}$	7
Waterbuck, sing-sing	68	$84^{6}/_{8}$	1	27	$36^{1}/_{4}$	7
Waterbuck, East African defassa	68	$87^{7}/_{8}$	1	27	35	7
Waterbuck, Ugandan defassa	NC	NC	NC	$33^{7}/_{8}$	$39^{1}/_{4}$	7
Waterbuck, Crawshay defassa	55	$74^{6}/_{8}$	1	25	$31^{1}/_{4}$	7
Waterbuck, Angolan defassa	ED	$75^{5}/_{8}$	1	24	$36^{1}/_{8}$	7

ED=editor's discretion; NC=no category; NE=no entry.

The Perfect Shot: Mini Edition for Africa

Animal	SCI			RW		
	Minimum	Record	Method	Minimum	Record	Method
Wildebeest, black or white-tailed	72	$96^2/_8$	6	$22^7/_8$	$29^3/_8$	13
Wildebeest, brindled gnu	NC	NC	NC	$28^1/_2$	$33^7/_8$	12
Wildebeest, blue	70	$96^4/_8$	5	NC	NC	NC
Wildebeest, Cookson	70	$94^5/_8$	5	NC	NC	NC
Wildebeest, Nyasa	64	$93^6/_8$	5	28	$33^1/_8$	12
Wildebeest, white-bearded	68	$94^1/_8$	5	28	32	12
Hartebeest, Cape/red	62	$80^5/_8$	1	23	$29^1/_2$	7
Hartebeest, Coke	50	73	1	$18^7/_8$	24	7
Hartebeest, Kenya highland	ED	$66^7/_8$	1	NC	NC	NC
Hartebeest, Neumann	51	$63^1/_8$	1	NC	NC	NC
Hartebeest, Swayne	ED	45	1	$16^7/_8$	$20^1/_4$	7
Hartebeest, tora	ED	NE	NE	$19^7/_8$	$22^7/_8$	7
Hartebeest, lelwel	60	$76^5/_8$	1	23	$27^5/_8$	7
Hartebeest, western	60	$77^2/_8$	1	$22^1/_2$	$28^3/_4$	7
Hartebeest, Lichtenstein	53	76	1	$18^1/_2$	$24^3/_8$	7
Hartebeest, Hunters	NC	NC	NC	23	$28^1/_2$	7

ED=editor's discretion; NC=no category; NE=no entry.

Animal	SCI			RW		
	Minimum	Record	Method	Minimum	Record	Method
Impala, East African	60	$77^6/_8$	1	$26^3/_8$	$36^1/_8$	7
Impala, southern	54	$76^4/_8$	1	$23^5/_8$	$31^7/_8$	7
Impala, Angolan/black-faced	ED	$67^7/_8$	1	$20^7/_8$	$26^3/_4$	7
Springbok, Kalahari	38	$50^2/_8$	1	14	$19^3/_8$	7
Springbok, Angolan	ED	$39^7/_8$	1	NC	NC	NC
Springbok, South African	30	$44^7/_8$	1	NC	NC	NC
Springbok, black	30	$44^1/_8$	1	NC	NC	NC
Springbok, white	28	$42^7/_8$	1	NC	NC	NC
Klipspringer	11	$16^{14}/_{16}$	1A	$4^1/_8$	$6^3/_8$	7
Bush Duiker, southern	11	$18^{10}/_{16}$	1A	$4^1/_2$	$7^1/_8$	7
Bush Duiker, Angolan	11	$15^1/_{16}$	1A	3	$6^1/_2$	7
Bush Duiker, East African	11	$15^{12}/_{16}$	1A	$3^7/_8$	$6^1/_8$	7
Bush Duiker, western	10	$15^2/_{16}$	1A	$3^3/_8$	$6^1/_4$	7
Duiker, Jentink	ED	$22^8/_{16}$	1A	5	$8^3/_8$	7
Duiker, yellow-backed	13	$22^2/_{16}$	1A	$4^1/_2$	$8^3/_8$	7
Duiker, Abbott	ED	$15^3/_{16}$	1A	3	$4^3/_8$	7

ED=editor's discretion; NC=no category; NE=no entry.

The Perfect Shot: Mini Edition for Africa

Animal	SCI			RW		
	Minimum	Record	Method	Minimum	Record	Method
Duiker, bay	5	$17^3/_{16}$	1A	$2^3/_8$	$4^3/_4$	7
Duiker, Peters	6	$18^8/_{16}$	1A	3	$5^3/_8$	7
Duiker, Weyns	ED	$14^5/_{16}$	1A	NC	NC	NC
Duiker, Gabon/white-bellied	ED	15	1A	$2^3/_4$	5	7
Duiker, black-fronted	ED	$14^2/_{16}$	1A	$2^1/_2$	$4^3/_4$	7
Duiker, red	ED	NE	1A	NC	NC	NC
Duiker, Ogilby	ED	$16^6/_{16}$	1A	$3^3/_8$	$4^7/_8$	7
Duiker, zebra	ED	$12^6/_{16}$	1A	1	$2^1/_2$	7
Duiker, black	ED	$16^6/_{16}$	1A	$2^3/_8$	$6^7/_8$	7
Duiker, Harvey red	6	$15^2/_{16}$	1A	$2^1/_2$	5	7
Duiker, Natal red	8	$13^2/_{16}$	1A	$2^1/_2$	$4^1/_8$	7
Duiker, Ruwenzori red	ED	NE	1A	NC	NC	NC
Duiker, red-flanked	7	$13^8/_{16}$	1A	$2^1/_2$	$4^1/_8$	7
Duiker, Ader	NE	NE	NE	1	$1^1/_2$	7
Duiker, Maxwell	ED	$8^{12}/_{16}$	1A	$1^1/_8$	$2^5/_8$	7
Duiker, blue	4	$8^{15}/_{16}$	1A	$1^3/_4$	$2^7/_8$	7

ED=editor's discretion; NC=no category; NE=no entry.

The Perfect Shot: Mini Edition for Africa

Animal	SCI			RW		
	Minimum	Record	Method	Minimum	Record	Method
Duiker, Simpson	NC	NC	NC	1⅛	NE	7
Hippo, common	50	88³/₁₆	12	29⅞	64½	5
Warthog	30	49¹⁰/₁₆	12	13	24	6
Crocodile, Nile	9'	17' 8"	16C	14	17	18

ED=editor's discretion; NC=no category; NE=no entry.

Records are according to *SCI Record Book of Trophy Animals*, Ed. X, Vol. 1, 2003; *Records of Big Game*, 25th edition, 1998.

Conversions: 1 inch = 2.54 centimeters; 1 pound = 454 grams.

See Appendix II and III for explanation of measurement methods.

The Perfect Shot: Mini Edition for Africa

Appendix II: Measurement methods used, Safari Club International

SCI started its measurement system in 1977 in Tucson, Arizona. In the beginning it was largely a book for club members only, but it has now grown well beyond this. Its measurement methods for African game are relatively simple. A book with listings of animal measurements and the hunters who have shot them is issued every few years. SCI currently (2002) has ten editions in print. We list only the SCI methods that are applicable to African animals in this book. (This is only a synopsis of the SCI system; for a full description, we refer you to the SCI Record Book of Trophy Animals.)

Method 1 (for animals with simple horns) — Length of horns (left and right) plus circumferences of horns at bases (left and right), to nearest $1/8$ inch.

Method 1A (for small animals with simple horns) — Length of horns (left and right) plus circumferences of horns at bases (left and right), to nearest $1/16$ inch.

Method 2 (for animals with spiraled horns) – Length of horns (left and right) along spiral ridge plus circumferences of horns at bases (left and right), to nearest $1/8$ inch.

Method 4 (for African buffalo) – From left tip to right tip of horns along bottom of horns plus width of each boss to nearest $1/8$ inch.

The Perfect Shot: Mini Edition for Africa

Method 5 (for common wildebeest) – From left tip to right tip of horns along bottom of horns across forehead plus circumference of boss of each horn to nearest $\frac{1}{8}$ inch.

Method 6 (for black wildebeest) – Start at horn tip, measure to the bottom of the first curve, come up behind to the top of the boss, cross the gap of the horns to the other boss and continue in a same manner to the other horn tip. Add to this the widths of both bosses.

Method 8 (for rhino) – Length of front horn plus circumference of front horn at base. Add to this length of rear horn plus circumference of rear horn at base, to nearest $\frac{1}{8}$ inch.

Method 12 (for hippo and warthog) – Length of both lower tusks on outer curve plus circumference of both tusks at largest place, to nearest $\frac{1}{16}$ inch.

Method 14 (for elephant) – Weight of left and right tusks to nearest $\frac{1}{2}$ pound.

Method 15 (for carnivores) – Length of skull plus width of skull to nearest $\frac{1}{16}$ inch.

Method 16C (for crocodiles) – Length of body, including tail, up over the top line of the body, to nearest $\frac{1}{2}$ inch.

Appendix III: Measurement methods used by Rowland Ward

Rowland Ward, owner of the most famous taxidermist studio of his time, started this measurement system in 1892 in London. The measurement methods are very simple; many require the length of only one antler or horn. A book with listings of animal measurements and the hunters who have shot them is issued every three to four years. RW currently (2002) has twenty-six editions in print. We list only the RW methods that are applicable to African animals in this book. Please note that RW requires a number of supplemental measurements that are not used in the ranking and, for reasons of brevity, are not listed here. (This is only a synopsis of the RW system; for a full description we refer you to Records of Big Game.*)*

Method 5 (for hippo) – Length of the longest lower tusk.

Method 6 (for warthog) – Length of the longest upper tusk.

Method 7 (for species with simple, unbranched horns) – Length of the longest horn along front curve.

Method 8 (for spiral-horned species) – Length of the longest horn along the spiral ridge.

Method 11 (for dwarf buffalo) – Length of the longest horn on outside curve.

Method 12 (for all other buffalo and common wildebeest) – Width of outside spread along straight line at right angles to the axis of the skull.

Method 13 (for black wildebeest) – Length of the longest horn. Measure by starting at the bottom of the boss, go with the grain of the horn to the tip.

Method 15 (for rhino) – Length of the longest horn measured along the front curve.

Method 16 (for elephant) – Weight of the single heaviest tusk.

Method 17 (for carnivores) – Length of skull added to width of skull.

Method 18 (for crocodiles) – Field measurement, before skinning. Pull the nose and tail to get them into a straight line (make sure crocodile is dead!). Then drive in pegs at the end of the nose and tail. Take the measurements between pegs and NOT following the line of the body, to nearest $1/4$ inch.

The Perfect Shot: Mini Edition for Africa

Appendix IV: Selected tracks

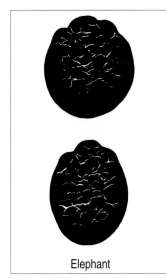

Elephant

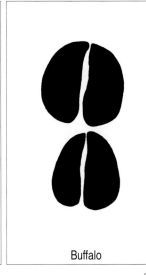

Buffalo

Hippopotamus

(Top: front foot; bottom: rear foot. Not to scale)

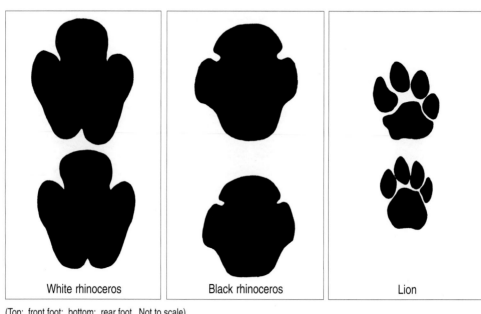

White rhinoceros | Black rhinoceros | Lion

(Top: front foot; bottom: rear foot. Not to scale)

The Perfect Shot: Mini Edition for Africa

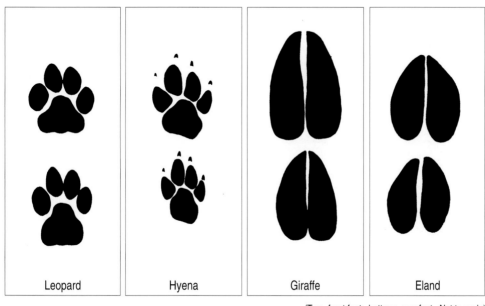

Leopard Hyena Giraffe Eland

(Top: front foot; bottom: rear foot. Not to scale)

The Perfect Shot: Mini Edition for Africa

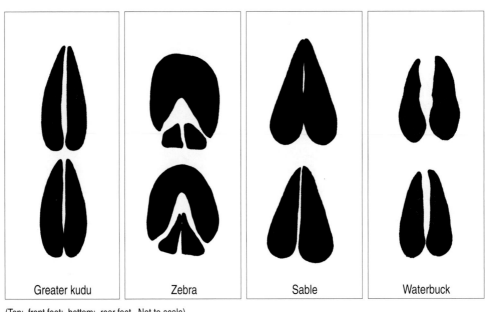

| Greater kudu | Zebra | Sable | Waterbuck |

(Top: front foot; bottom: rear foot. Not to scale)

The Perfect Shot: Mini Edition for Africa

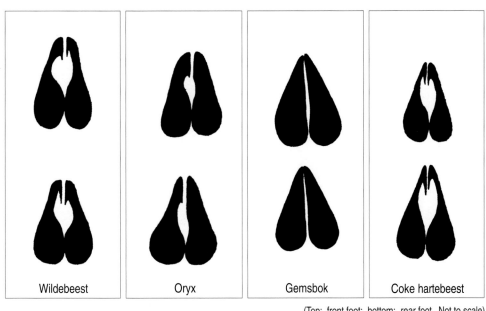

| Wildebeest | Oryx | Gemsbok | Coke hartebeest |

(Top: front foot; bottom: rear foot. Not to scale)

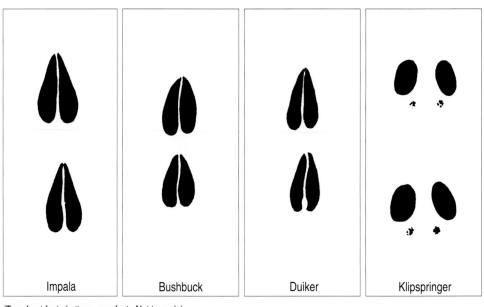

(Top: front foot; bottom: rear foot. Not to scale)

| Impala | Bushbuck | Duiker | Klipspringer |

The Perfect Shot: Mini Edition for Africa